THE LONGED FOR LONGED FOR

THE LONGED FOR LONGED FOR
© Sibani Sen / Cathexis Northwest Press

No part of this book may be reproduced without written permission of the publisher or author, except in reviews and articles.

First Printing: 2025

ISBN: 978-1-952869-95-2

Cover Painting by Avinav Cariens; Cover Design by Audeep Cariens.
Editing & Design by C. M. Tollefson
Cathexis Northwest Press
cathexisnorthwestpress.com

THE LONGED FOR LONGED FOR

SIBANI SEN

Cathexis Northwest Press

This is a collection of poems voiced from the perspective of the migrant, the marginal and the estranged. It contains elegy, sorrow and ghost whispers that accompany the experiences of exile, loss, indentureship, and death. It emerges from my own history and ancestry in the East and West Indies, from mixed diasporas and migratory aspirations. Though these poems are rooted in my life, I hope to convey the Möbius loop of longing familiar to us all: the bind we can get into of wanting an elsewhere that is really a nowhere, or yearning for someone beyond reach—an absence that gives our lives meaning. At times, in these poems, I look for relief and reckoning in the inner life of the psyche and the imagination, in the bravery of love and the restitution of art, as well as finding succor in the natural world. In other moments, the lack of consolation brings wisdom. Even if the parted father and daughter will never reconcile, and there is no remedy for alienation, nor any redemption for a history of enslavement and its stolen futures, there remains for me, in each of these poems, an evolution into greater resiliency, and an awakening into the boundlessness of life. Although these poems are borderland elegies, they are modes of keening, desiring, grasping and, especially, surviving, that are universal. Existence, in these poems, is the condition of longing, with an invitation to solidarity, since we are all migrants in time.

FOR SUMON AND NILAN

Table of Contents

(I)

Maroon	1
Self-Portrait in the Cane Field	2
Planting the Rice Field	3
Interrogation	4
Chronicle for my Descendants	5
Dead-wing	6
Solitaire	7
Ars Poetica as Lost Daughter	8
Oracle for the Indentured Ancestors	9
Self-Portrait Unrequited	10
Ars Poetica as Drudge	11
Passing Through	12
Rorschach	13
End Note	14
Tally for the Turn	15
Father At Sea	16
The Contagion Is You	17
The Cherry Tree is Heavy with Blossoms	18

(II)

The Longed For, Longed For	23
We Have Come Through Strife	24
Dirge	25
In Father's Atelier	26
Diptych	27
Life Sentence	28
Nightcap	29
Transient	30
Migrant's Gloaming	31
And afterwards, like Philomela, I too will Sing	32
Late Shift	33
Migrant Memory	34
Ancestral Ghosts	35
After Grief, Renewal	36
Inamorata	37
Flock mind	38
Words lie under the tongue	39
Afterword	40

"heard melodies are sweet but those unheard are sweeter"

— John Keats

(I)

Maroon

(A slave's riddle)

Under the vernacular sun
I tally cane and gold,
I, raconteur of the tannic hills.

Mandarins in castled groves
Cultivate calendula blooms
Upon my back.

Red sill and coal
Suss out my thousand eyes.
I lash time,

Shiver in my
Slurry skin; pitched, flailed,
I prepare the vestal.

I bring it level to the light:
Brim, flow, one
Immaculate, everlasting life.

Self-Portrait in the Cane Field

I do not want
so much to think
as find my twin
in me, still thirsty.

So, drown this hour
in the velvet air—
dim stars blink,
lumpish in my mind.

No space between
the field and furrow;
we plant vapors,
we stave thought.

Vast motions thick,
long stalks rustle.
The cane bends over me:
orisons of quietude.

Planting the Rice Field

the geometry is the simple
series of patterns my father felt
(an ocean squared
the orchard's perspective)

        bent in repose
             containing the
             connecting the

grains as they murmur up
to the surface screen like a
vision of another country

      to feel
          in angles
          each urge

seen under a greater angle
appear greater, under a lesser angle less,
under equal angles appear equal:

      (urgent) try to
          know when
          to fit

Interrogation

in that life I was unerring

so there was no indirection

as a child taught by instruments and the blood helped on

the limits of my skin were explained to me

the way shoulders will crack when bent behind the back

the way teeth knuckled out can topple flat

and one can feel submarine when hung by the heel

examined for what cannot be known

my success was always thwarted

nails sometimes shed on their own

undulations of white in the eyes

would frighten outright

I grew

Chronicle for My Descendants

Some other time they will want to know the way we looked.
How we saw the city domes exuding an air of malcontent,
As if shadows fell across the pavements deeper
Than what you or I may mean to each other. I imagine it.
Words might fill it up with scruff and fledge of feelings.
A longing to get underneath the surfaces to some
Uncommon knowledge, to scour the present moment
With a new sense of who they are. They may be uneasy
With us in the future, like people were with the first films:
Frightened of ghosts that appear and disappear, resurrected
On a wall, shape-shifting till no distinctness remained.
Till whatever they touched was out of reach.

Dead-wing

Father speaks from the desert.

one day you will go to the desert
to see birds tending the blanched bones
nesting in clear sockets

these birds migrate at night
where do they go?

their sad cries
the miraculous beating of wings
they cease to exist here

each wish is real then
each wish leaves the face of the earth

they store the light that was lost:
un-wing it tonight
fill the dark with eyes

I must think of my desire
winged this way

when they seize me
breath and wing-beat
you say I chose it.

Solitaire

We make ourselves, or we make each self
new; that is the mortal ken—no other
longing will suffice. Destined

to remain versions uncollected—not grass, not herd,
nor roe—made multitude, yet resisting communion.
No, not the school of silver fish nor the flock's

attenuated arrow. Yet the singularity is spent,
sinking like the theoretical soul, the lone
outsized singling out, weary as the sun to see

his thirsty offspring, at each diurnal turning.
The dark glows with the lightning swarm.
Time's eternal maw is below, above, the solitary dove.

Ars Poetica as Lost Daughter

She rubbed her undersoles
With camphor oil and thistle seed
To chafe away the first bite.

Here at the bottom
With the jail-kooks and lies
The blue of her slide begins.

She hops around and mirrors
Flash. She dances, she sings.
She coos with eyes, she crows.

Her spiny bones revert
To bitter, tearless sighs
Hungry to be known.

oracle for the indentured ancestors

now, like a revenant, I
reap the harvest
of loneliness, faded memories
carried across black waters
through the accordion of time:
faces stilled, unnamed voices silenced.
the winds blow, blowing
tomorrows away. each inveterate voyager
sundered and sought for, I claim.

Self-Portrait Unrequited

There are nights when
winds make waves in the brain
without surging into thought.

I do not know that particle called love but
I imagine a lover's kiss—light flits sullen on the eyelid like
mollusks floating in the deep, their own conclusions momentary.

Years weep, the rain roars
Underwater. Quiver for
Softness, yet succumb to an impenetrable pearl.

Ars Poetica as Drudge

In quiet moments
The snow seems loud
Night dreams racket
At dawn, in the attic, the sun feels garish
Parading his harlequin colors about,
Bleeding heart in a plastic sky.
Below the traffic shuffles like muffled laughter.
Another day wakens to another ruse,
Kaleidoscopes turning, turning,
Smearing the farce of me into the farce of you.
We playthings and fools
Painting scenes for sycophants.
Everyone sees to forget,
Forgets to see, and the whim
Of the moment is to be furtive,
Or rage under siege—I carry it, unwieldy as it is.

Passing Through

Borne down by gifts and death berates me.
The measure of each, its mewling for its maker
All these intimations, amock, tutor.

Look, look up. Not this ceiling, but that common view,
A salient sky, a sea-teeming horizon goads;
History's hell space, memory fleeting yet wrought,

Drawn up into work-a-day writ, a tamp in the gut
Or secret mote for tomorrow, some grain husk
Flashing, peripheral, fleet incandescence.

Rorschach

Draw it from my skin:
so, the forest splits and leaves
fall this way mottled, that way
they cling burnt to
the vulnerable trees. Let go.

My inkblot, my tiny seraphim.

I found her in my breast pocket,
she sings to me in wonder.
I sing to her in pity;
lead me to the trees with
their too much electric hues.

My memento, shadow twin.

There is nothing to accept.
She is docile when I slip her out
poked and she balls up in my hand.
Here is my angel who is not
Chosen. Bring me in.
I may not bring you out.

End Note

In your mouth, a ruined content.
Everything dies in it: fruits, fish, language and lovers
A week's short span gushed you out in technicolor:
Season I refuse.

Already I grasp this last shoot of summer,
Trodden vines, some ghost seeds rattling
The husk. You used to dip like a gardener parting

Brambles, sweaty amidst the plumbago.
Now blood blooms like late chrysanthemum in a midden.
Heated gaze dims. Fall powders into dust.
Skin now marmoreal. I kiss air.

Tally for the Turn

Even when the gay forsythia limbs the snow,
and bloodroot drapes the long dead soil
or the cherry blooms blush in the lengthening dusks
and pink dogwoods lip the slate slattern sky,
March rains mute it all for me.
The new growth of the naked wintering trees
unfurl their sheen. All at once the daffodils dapple the muddy
runnels, crocus and trillium scatter in the stubble midden. Light
is surly and wavers still. The magnolia ravishes for a single
day. Quince and redbud release their gaudy grille. How
to live now after such solemn sleep, with much lost, and more
still hurting? The sap rushes. The season stings. Awash in
pollen and the verdant skin of spring—despite the dead—
the trees insist. The green galls and I am
shocked awake again, bereaved leaf, yes, helpless to resist.

Father At Sea

In the body of the daughter is the body of the father
Shall we measure time's consolation or betrayal?

You touch my face tracing tears
Is this salt of the earth, sieve of our memory?

I pull you in and we are buffeted by the waves.
Can we hold each other fast in the shifting sands?

It was always a trade in even tension.
Was it the balance found in dreams or departures?

Did you have to leave in order to arrive in me?
Did you find me in what you had lost?

The weeds in the water tangle our bodies together.
Is this your heart where once was your mind?

How you loved your seeking.
Who knows that ardent hunger now?

Where can the wilderness find
her immortal beauty except in your eye?

You see a dream in me
but when will I see you again?

The Contagion Is You

Father's last words.

I have to live though I died twice
        that day of the crash—

a stranger's blessing in a curse
        you said—it made me

stronger until it happened again
        this time it was all within

when the contagion claimed
        a smile's stealth breath

a secret you had waiting
        for me to discover a disappearing

act you practiced all my life
        so often I never thought

it could ever be real.
        Don't worry you said

I will be ok, when you meant to say
        you will be ok, without me (trick mirror).

There is a meridian here
        I cannot live where the sun never sets.

Cruelest sting
        oh, bird without wings

Find me in that valiant true night.
        Let me see you again.

The Cherry Tree is Heavy with Blossoms

I look for you everywhere
but the street is full of strangers
who look at me and say nothing.

How did you ever love this inhospitable earth?
How do any of us? I eat the dirt I walk on.
I breathe the air of death.

In a dream your face is a mirage of stars that wink
one brightness at a time, snuffed out
and ravaged by the sun.

You must have known this was coming.
You must have known that grudging mother of us all
would come back to fetch you.

The dead line the street, the cherry tree heavy with blossoms
The day bludgeons bright with desire.
It strikes me like a snake who slithers on forever.

(II)

The Longed For Longed For

Someday l will go to the wall
Where you leaned at last—
I will see your bowed and burnished head,
Silvered curls and milky eyes.
I will hear your voice rattle,
Scolding and sweet.

In the far district of my child's sight
I will stand a long time
Out there on the ledge
In the vast depository, in the land of legend
I will feel lost, uncertain and at home.

We Have Come Through Strife

Sleepless, we trace constellations on skin,
milky tracks, sheen, and in your eyes

contrails of that ascending feeling you'd had
when we first met, 'lords of our own faces.'

Arm-in-arm we stare out into air rustling with
wishes, moth-struck, swept into a kind of waiting

like a season's turning, or what weather feels like.
The desire to no longer fall into ourselves,

prickling at the neck, loosening hips with the look
of years. We stare as if to learn by heart

our own baring. Nights bring on that intent,
the thought that some new feeling will appear, and

what we already know will vanish.
So, the leaves, or a leaf, will tell us much.

The trees may stir, magnificent like
your hair, silvering. In a moment,

in the darkness, I will reach for your hand
wondering, is there any strangeness left?

Dirge

Paladin of a hundred years
Dispute me in your corps

Like phases of the planetary sun.
The self-same coursing

The pulse of the scriptorium
Here, learned page by page.

The leaves bleed, each a season's
Surfeit: wrung, gleaning, sore.

I write of the eternal rusting
Glistening, yes, cleansing.

In that dissent mine dissembles.
The promenade of hues

Of penumbral rushes,
Stanchions of light.

It singularly stirs the oil in me,
Seeks a brighter pressing

For tracing immortelles.
Culling the earth, icy lancets sting.

The book of love and loss
Winters in the heart, grace-struck.

In Father's Atelier

I remember you
Not a face, not a voice, but
A presence—no likeness,
No moving picture will allay
That shimmer—the warmth
A steady bar against my own
Doleful amnesia,
Habits obdurate, you
Cutting stone

And love split me, found me
Reproached me. Oh, is there
Any sting sweeter than
The lash of confession
The desperate spleen
Beneath. Lothario to myself.
Steady, you will not have me
Outrun you, that infinite vision,
My infinite sleep.

Diptych

An old man sits at the window,
the sun glints silver in his hair
framing his eyes with silver lines
he glows like a skin-peeled fruit
wrinkled flesh, soft in the fading light.

We traveled far across oceans, across lands.

I recognize myself in his face, the pointed chin, with
his rounded eyes, legs outstretched along the sill, as
he sprawls still, holding easy within himself the
question of ages, the why-ever-how wonder.

Far along the inhospitable earth, the limned light.

At the window looking out, the world looking
in, his twin reflected, rippled in the glass,
a warp to fill the passing hours, days gather
 a recollection of being, of bone.

Over straits, far into unsuspecting weather.

Those long legs were limber,
long days of laughter, a hunger to
hurry in the world, and scry the small dreaming toy
soldiers, balls and sticks, whoops, whistles,
so slyly I barely caught a glimpse.

How far, for another tether in the rush?

Old man remember—the walks
we had along the river in the golden hour
the flagstone bridge, meadow grass aflame,
the mocking bird's call to-wit, to-wit
bewildering—the river, through the window,
the light. Time, come as you will.

Come find me far from memory, ravenous.

Life Sentence

There is nothing you can say to make it better—
Lucretius had the sinking feeling too

though he knew some clam shells never shut
drifting in and out of dream.

No, it's not mortality I mean either, for
Lucretius or the clam. It's not the spider eggs

in their sac waiting to scatter-hatch, pincers and all.
It's not even their compulsions, feeling for its sake

that "we live dependent on each other."
Nor the diggers squelching in the sand

smattered with patches of morning light,
mining the composure of the ancients,
bodies bent raking, forgetting they are bodies,
eyes squinted, mouths open without a musical note

unable to help anything
that requires helping at all.

Nightcap

Love, ugly,
returns me to this
slight, a touch today,
tomorrow nothing. After that
Sunday, when no one knows
what happens next.

Love, alluvial,
spent the night.
I felt— prayers, riots,
ruined houses.
I dug the grounds
up and told nobody.

But love taller
than in my dreams
hung little beasts
dim with cravings
as birds passed by
vaster than the universe.

Transient

Elsewhere I sift through
the static of memory without antennae
the smell of urine under the causeway
the tree at the bus stop that faintly blossoms

with yellow enough to remind me
the pigeons are mating, or step in
guano stickier than usual in
a land of evanescence.

At this hour of the day do this, at that
hour of the day go there: the billboard
that told me is now blank. I am a mime
to whom each motion is a secret from myself.

Migrant's Gloaming

Shiftless, I go canoodling the melons,
hirsute and lumbering, the weather of my mind
hungry. Among the trees, now and then,
fruit bats—my agnostic angels—wrangle with me
for a bite. The savor of it cuts the loss of tomorrows.
A hammer bird sings in the leaves. Pomegranate seeds
gleam as lightening gleams in the grass trees.
Winds hang eglantine in the eaves baffling the sun
ray's drift, and now, a doppelganger of lighted air.
A bee-stung sunset at dusk and dust rising to meet the rain.
For a moment, purple phlox bloodies these jewel petal eyes
like a joy one can't intend. I feel the generous ease of this moment,
its wide embrace open and unutterable. Then, it is evening.

And afterwards, like Philomela, I too will Sing

Wild jasmine, white runes
Trace the shuttle of time.
Past moonlight, suddenly

An angel descends sweet-throated,
Soft-winged, alight in the lush bush
Limned native of the night.

What small missal is this?
A tinkling annunciation
Vespers for a solitary

Pax with boughs, beasts, air,
An inner exile in the world,
Sings unconcerned.

Blind, I hear that beauty.
Cruel, individual notes
Not to fathom, but bear.

Momentary ruse
Eternal muse, coiled
Unerringly in each other.

Late Shift

Driving home after
midnight when traffic
grows silent and
horses remember plains.

I think, like them, I am ready
to always be ready
though time takes over
in the end.

Long roads now
seamed asphalt and tar paper,
slick in the new morning;
a smoky green dawn

lights up slowly, lights littered
cigarette-ends, wind-tossed cellophane-wrap,
toll-booths rising above the fog,
further than they appear.

Panes of brightened glass
frame the road work crew,
their jumpsuits blooming
amidst the silver slipped coins,

slot-bound like me
heading towards
the brightening roust
persistent as day.

Migrant Memory

Late November when you have the chance,
Drive out here to the shore,
Drive towards the sunset when leaves are
Burnt-curled, the few left, easily shaken,
Winter light disappearing into dark.

Turn your windows down,
Feel the clearing air, see
Tree-shapes rushing past like ink,
Trailing past you, words leaving you dry.
When you get to the beach, a space opens up—

Pitch upon pitch at the craggy edge where the ancestors
Arrived. If the moon's new, the bucket sky domes over you,
Punctured by the bright foil of distant stars.
They saw them too. Salt seeps into skin, ocean air
Prickles the neck, tautens hips.

Their black hair unraveled in the waves,
And dark skin enveloped in the night.
Under the benediction of those shorn, bereft
trees fledged on the cliffsides feel their longing
for the season's renewal, despite the wintering now.

Ancestral Ghosts

At the top of the stairs
out of the top-most window,
I look out to the beach and feel
suddenly indistinct.

The weak glow of cloud-milked stars
light wave tips and shoreline sedged in
tendrils of surf—there shadows glisten. The tilt
of a seeming torso, taut like a god's, born

of the original sea. I look and find
I cannot hold on to my name, once more
thrown back onto myself and the inevitable
years of making now unmaking, the ache

of release closed in by this small lit window,
inescapable straits of tumult, restive, seeking.
Across the sea, where it is always new, flung,
now flown by, this ache asks of me again.

After Grief, Renewal

The first day of Spring.
I make love. I submit to a light
dance, a March festival.
The rains stop. Lightning.
The rains begin again. Dawn's pink tin holds
the dark side of the moon faintly—the bright
side of the moon a scythe or pinched navel
where all creation tents over me, over me.
My children and I walk hand in hand.
Grass grows neon and sweet.
A sharp wind whets the scent of blossoms.
Worms drowned in sidewalk puddles squelch underfoot.
I did not want you to be other than you are.

Inamorata

Awake in the darkness
that loves me. How it wonders
and yearns as I yearn for the light.

I hear a coyote calling at the bridge.
I feel the lonely howl in my heart.
There is bitterness:

an asking into the night—where
are you, my friend? Fled
with the sinking of the sun.

Warp of the sun, scythe of the sun.
The darkness seeks. Do not
keep me long my friend.

The scent of time and memory,
the sight of insight in those
animal eyes. The snake uncoiled,

the leaping frogs and flies
do not yield to me. In a dream
further afield, windows glow,

doors close to me. Feel the force
of that beast, the last are the first,
the night weepers give way

to the light eaters, and the dark
ravishes, ripens, releases
world without end.

flock mind

expand, connect as dart tip
of bird; if corkscrew updrafts
blow off course, reform,
pivot each part, beak to tail.

in the arrowed air the dip
depends on instinct, expectation.
invisible currents join each migrant.
eddies counter, the flanks hold.

words lie under the tongue

like the primordial breath. thou art
that. beneath a mirror sink the stone
in the still, scatter fish
muddy the deep turtle ledge.

silence is heavy. how long can it last?
some days stoke the birds to suddenly
swarm up—songs unleashed; or the scrape of leaves
blown all at once, shape a tree. at dusk

one is grateful for the chance to have not said
what birds and fish will never know:
the world is a vitrine of beatitudes;
the glass edge felt and forgotten.

Afterword

Your face, Father, aglow at the crossing
Of my sleep—this is how
Dreamtime resurrects you.

I never noticed how you kept
Yourself firmly bound within,
Like camouflage that hides

The serpent in the grass. Memory
Will entwine us in concealment.
We can pretend. Recall

How I told you the once-upon-a-times are
My favorite? My skin prickles
—The snake reposed, suddenly strikes

—Here now, then gone again,
Hurtling into the deep recesses of tomorrow,
Seven ages ahead, six extinctions away.

I wonder how to survive? How
Lonely will it be in this aftermath
With only the dead to shape my smile?

Acknowledgements

Book of Matches, Lit: "The Longed For, Longed For"

Border Arts:beyond the barrier anthology: "Dead Wing" (originally published as "Dead-Winged")

Global Quarantine Museum: "The Contagion is You"

The Hopper: "Tally for the Turn"

Main Street Rag: "Life Sentence"

Nixes Mate Review: "End Note"

Off the Coast: "Planting the Rice Field" & "Self-Portrait Unrequited"

Pangyrus: "The Cherry Tree is Heavy with Blossoms"

Saranac Review: "Father At Sea"

SWWIM: "Maroon"

The Tampa Review: "Dirge"

Sibani Sen's poetry has appeared in a variety of publications including *Off the Coast, Saranac Review, Tampa Review, Rogue Agent* and *SWIMM*. She has worked on many collaborative multimedia projects including exhibits at the Harvard Hutchins Center, the Concord Museum, and the Green Street Studio in Massachusetts. She has also co-created experimental performances at the Public Theater and with Movement Without Borders in New York. Sibani's current work includes forthcoming poetry and translations of the pre-modern Indian poet Bharatchandra. She teaches creative writing and history and can be found at sibanisen.com

Also Available from Cathexis Northwest Press:

<u>Something To Cry About</u>
by Robert Krantz

<u>Suburban Hermeneutics</u>
by Ian Cappelli

<u>God's Love Is Very Busy</u>
by David Seung

<u>that one time we were almost people</u>
by Christian Czaniecki

<u>Fever Dream/Take Heart</u>
by Valyntina Grenier

<u>The Book of Night & Waking</u>
by Clif Mason

<u>Dead Birds of New Zealand</u>
by Christian Czaniecki

<u>The Weathering of Igneous Rockforms in High-Altitude Riparian Environments</u>
by John Belk

<u>If A Fish</u>
by George Burns

<u>How to Draw a Blank</u>
by Collin Van Son

<u>En Route</u>
by Jesse Wolfe

<u>sky bright psalms</u>
by Temple Cone

<u>Moonbird</u>
by Henry G. Stanton

<u>southern athiest. oh, honey</u>
by d. e. fulford

<u>Bruises, Birthmarks & Other Calamities</u>
by Nadine Klassen

<u>Wanted: Comedy, Addicts</u>
by AR Dugan

<u>They Curve Like Snakes</u>
by David Alexander McFarland

<u>the catalog of daily fears</u>
by Beth Dufford

<u>Shops Close Too Early</u>
by Josh Feit

Vanity Unfair and Other Poems
by Robert Eugene Rubino

Destructive Heresies
by Milo E. Gorgevska

Bodies of Separation
by Chim Sher Ting

The Night with James Dean and Other Prose Poems
by Allison A. deFreese

About Time
by Julie Benesh

Suspended
by Ellen White Rook

The Unempty Spaces Between
by Louis Efron

Quomodo probatur in conflatorio
by Nick Roberts

Suspended
by Ellen White Rook

Call Me Not Ishmael but the Sea
by J. Martin Daughtry

Wild Evolution
by Naomi Leimsider

Coming To Terms
by Peter Sagnella

Acta
by Patrick Wilcox

Honeymoon Shoes
by Valyntina Grenier

Practising Ascending
by Nadine Hitchiner

Home Visit
by Michal Rubin

LA CIUDAD EN TI: THE CITY WITHIN YOU
by Karla Marrufo
Translated from the Spanish by Allison A. deFreese

Resin in the Milky Way
by Amanda Rabaduex

Bone Hunting
by Trinity Catlin

Muskets for the Bear Problem
by Andrew Whitmer

Self-Portraits as a Reddening Sky
by Samuel Gilpin

Desert
by Eric Larsh

Leaving the Religion of Self-Harm
by Bailey Blumenstock

Fractured Symphony
by Andi Myles

La dulzura de los naufragios: The Sweetness of Shipwrecks
by Karla Marrufo
Translated from the Spanish by Allison A. deFreese

Love & Fear
by Henry G. Stanton

Sunlight Later
by Jo Matthews

The Longed For Longer For
by Sibani Sen

Brood
by Kelly Granito

Bleeding Ghosts
by Lara Chamoun

As Jaguars Dreamed On The Earth's Dark Face
by Clif Mason

Cathexis Northwest Press

www.ingramcontent.com/pod-product-compliance
Lightning Source LLC
Chambersburg PA
CBHW020443090526
44586CB00045B/813